Issi Noho

Also by Keith Chatfield in Piccolo

Issi Pandemonium

Keith Chatfield

Issi Noho

Illustrated by Edward C. Standon

A Piccolo Book
Pan Books in association with
William Heinemann

First published 1974 by William Heinemann Ltd
This edition published simultaneously by
Pan Books Ltd, Cavaye Place, London SW10 9PG,
in association with William Heinemann Ltd
2nd printing 1975

ISBN 0 330 24009 9

Printed in Great Britain by
Richard Clay (The Chaucer Press) Ltd, Bungay, Suffolk

Contents

Chapter 1

The stranger in Coppins Wood

"Excuse me, but I suppose you wouldn't have such a thing as a bamboo shoot about you?" asked a tiny voice very politely.

Andrew Martin swung round startled. It had been so quiet since Sally and Neil ran off to hide, and Andrew was waiting for the call of "READY!" which was the signal for him to begin searching for them. He'd worked out roughly where Sally was hiding, but after that his mind wandered a bit. For one thing it looked like rain, and for another it was almost tea-time. He felt particularly hungry and was half-way through a delicious slice of cottage loaf spread with a thick layer of creamy butter and . . .

bamboo shoot!?

Andrew stared at the creature in front of him. It . . . it . . . looked like a panda!

"No, I didn't think you would have," said the tiny voice sadly. "Bamboo shoots don't seem to be in very great supply around here."

"I . . . I'm not sure I even know what a . . . what a bamboo shoot looks like," stammered Andrew, his eyes fixed on the panda. Yes, it definitely was a panda, and in the middle of Coppins Wood as well. Andrew couldn't believe his eyes.

"Well, I shall trouble you no further," said the panda politely, and he turned to go.

"READY!" yelled Sally from her hiding place.

"Here, don't go," Andrew called out. "I'm sorry I haven't a bamboo shoot, but I do have a licorice shoelace." He dug deeply into his right-hand pocket and took out the licorice, hastily peeling off two large pieces of tissue handkerchief, a conker, and a picture of his favourite footballer. He held the licorice out at arm's length and the panda ambled over to take it.

"I say, aren't you a panda?" asked Andrew.

"Yes, that's right," said the panda, with a mouth full of licorice. "What are you?"

"What am I?" cried Andrew. "I'm a boy, of course. I'm a big boy too. I'm seven

and three-quarters, you know."

"You're a very strange little boy," remarked the panda, who by now was cultivating a very strong liking for licorice.

"READY!" called Sally.

"What do you mean – strange?" asked Andrew indignantly. "You're the one who's strange. Whoever heard of a panda roaming about in the woods in England before, asking for bamboo shoots?"

"Oh, so that's where I am, in England," said the panda. "No wonder you're such a strange little boy. Where I come from all the little boys have a yellow skin and almond-shaped eyes and black hair. You've got fair hair and blue eyes and brown spots all over your face. You look strange to me," said the panda frankly.

"READY, READY, READY!" called Neil impatiently.

"Now look here." Andrew was getting a little cross. "I can't help having fair hair and blue eyes and freckles. Lots of English boys do. You like me well enough to eat all my licorice anyway, and you're . . ."

"Have you any more licorice? It's very tasty," remarked the panda.

"No I haven't. And don't interrupt. It's very rude," said Andrew sharply. "Now you've made me forget what I was saying."

"ARE YOU COMING OR NOT!" Sally shouted.

"I'm sure I didn't want to make you angry," said the panda. He sounded truly sorry as he turned to walk back into the woods.

Andrew suddenly felt silly at losing his temper over such a small thing. It was obvious that the panda had not meant to be rude.

"I'm not really cross," he called, trying hard to think of something to say before the panda disappeared amongst the trees. "Where do you live?"

The panda stopped. "Very near here," he said. "It's a very nice little residence. Not large, you know, but quite big enough for one. Would you like to see it?"

"Yes please," said Andrew eagerly. "Here, I say, what on earth are you doing in Coppins Wood?"

"It's all my father's fault really," explained the panda as he began his rather ungainly amble through the thicket. "Travel broadens the mind and it's about time you travelled and broadened a bit, he kept on telling me. Then he gave me this pouch." The panda indicated a leather pouch hanging from a cord round his neck. "Learn how to use the contents of this pouch properly, he told me, and you might even get to England one day. But I never expected to make it on my very first attempt."

"How did you get here?" asked Andrew.

"That's just it," said the panda. "There was this blinding flash and an enormous puff of green smoke and . . . ah!" The panda broke off what he was saying as they came to a clearing. "Here we are."

The panda's residence was indeed little. It looked like a sturdy wooden packing case covered with branches and leaves to camouflage it.

"It's actually a very sturdy wooden packing case which I've covered with branches and leaves to camouflage it," confirmed the panda.

"Is that your name over the doorway?" asked Andrew.

"Oh . . . er . . . yes," said the panda, eyeing the writing intently. "Er . . . have they spelt it correctly?"

"I–S–S–I, N–O–H–O," Andrew spelt out. "What a funny name, Issi Noho. It sounds Chinese."

"Well, of course it does," said the panda, "that's where I come from – China."

Actually no one had ever called him by name before but he liked the sound of it so much that he suddenly decided he wanted a name just like the one written above his front door.

"Would you mind saying my name again? It sounds funny pronounced by an English boy," he said.

"Issi Noho," said Andrew.

"Mm . . . Issi Noho," repeated the panda. "Yes, I like it. I mean I like the way you pronounce it. You can call me Issi if you like. What's your name?"

"Andrew Martin," said Andrew. "You can call me Andrew."

"I hope we shall be good friends," said Issi, and then he added, "I suppose you're quite sure you haven't any more licorice?"

"Quite sure," said Andrew, "but since we're friends I shall bring some more licorice for you as soon as I've had my tea."

"Come in for a minute. I'll show you round," said Issi. He stooped down and was about to step inside when a loud scream made him straighten up so quickly that he hit his head on the top of the doorway with a thud.

"Ooh . . . ah . . . ooh!"

As he fell backwards, clutching his head in his paws, Sally's frightened face peeped out from his house. Issi had discovered Sally's hiding place.

Poor Sally, she had been snugly crouching inside the packing case when she heard voices. A big bubble of excitement tingled in her tummy as she waited for Andrew to peep in and find her. She hardly dared look. The tingling bubble was about to burst into a loud giggle when suddenly, "OUCH!"

She saw two big black patched eyes staring at her. She was just about to scream again when she looked out and saw Andrew.

"Andrew, Andrew!" she cried. "What is it? Whatever is it?"

"It's not an 'it', he's a panda and his name is Issi. I think he's hurt. Come on, he won't bite you," said Andrew, running over to where the panda lay on the ground.

At that moment Neil burst into the clearing. He had grown tired of waiting and Sally's scream sounded just like the excitement he needed. He stopped dead in his tracks at the strange sight of Andrew kneeling on the ground nursing Issi's head on his lap.

"It's a panda and its name is Issi,"

explained Sally.

"What's wrong with it?" asked Neil advancing slowly.

"He banged his head because my silly sister screamed," said Andrew in disgust.

"Well, I wasn't expecting a panda to come to find me was I?" said Sally.

"I think he's got compulsion," said Andrew.

"You mean concussion, goof," said Sally. "I've learnt all about these things in the Brownies. I'll just see if I can find his pulse. Mm . . . well," she added after a moment. "His heart's still beating. As long as he keeps on breathing he'll be all right."

"That's silly," said Andrew. "Of course he'll be all right if he keeps on breathing!"

"I mean we must make sure that nothing chokes him. He mustn't swallow any chewing gum, or false teeth or anything."

"Well I've never heard of a panda with false teeth before," said Andrew in disgust. "Look, I wonder what that is." He pointed to a strangely patterned leather pouch hanging from a cord round Issi's neck.

"I don't know, but there's something important inside – he was just starting to tell me." Andrew put out a finger to touch it.

"Don't touch!" commanded Sally. "That's his private property. Andrew, what is he doing here? How did he get to Coppins Wood?"

"I don't know," said Andrew, "he was prattling on about blinding flashes and puffs of green smoke but he didn't finish his story. He lives in that old packing case where you were hiding. That's his name over the doorway – Issi Noho."

Sally went over to inspect. "Issi Noho," she said, pushing back the camouflage of overhanging branches and leaves. "It doesn't say anything of the sort," she cried. "It says –

THIS SIDE UP
USE NO HOOKS

It's just that the other letters were all covered up by the branches and only the middle ones could be seen!"

"Gosh," said Andrew, "the crafty old panda. He told me it was his name."

"Don't let's say anything," said Sally. "Issi Noho quite suits him and he's got to have a name. I'll put the branches back just as I found them."

Issi stirred. "Oh my head, my head!" he moaned.

"Issi!" cried Andrew. "Are you all right?"

"You were hiding in my house. You made me jump," said Issi, looking straight at Sally.

"I – I know. I'm very sorry," stammered Sally. "I didn't know it was your house."

"Don't mention it," said Issi. "You're very welcome to call any time you like. That's my name over the doorway," he added, proudly pointing at the letters ISSI NOHO. "What's your name?"

"Sally Martin," said Sally.

"And mine's Neil Mackenzie," Neil chimed in.

"Sally and Neil," said Issi. "That makes two more friends I've made today." And then he added, "You will be my friends, won't you?"

"Of course we shall!" cried the children. They were bubbling with excitement. This was the strangest thing that had happened to them in their whole lives. But even the strangest and most exciting things cannot stop tummies rumbling when they're hungry, and Andrew's was reminding him that it was time for food.

"Here, we really must go home. It's ages past teatime," he exclaimed. "Mum will be furious. We'll come back straight after."

"Er . . . you won't forget to bring some licorice with you when you come back, will you?" asked Issi in his politest voice.

"There's a word missing," said Sally firmly.

Issi looked puzzled.

"She means p–l–e–a–s–e," explained Andrew.

"Please?" said Issi.

"If you want someone to do something you must always say 'please'. That's something you have to remember." Sally's voice was slightly scolding.

"Oh come on, Sal," said Andrew, "the sooner we go the sooner we can come back."

"Don't forget my licorice," said Issi.

"PLEASE!" shouted Sally, as she ran after her brother.

"Oh yes – please!"

Everything was suddenly very quiet in the clearing after all the chatter and excitement. Issi looked at the lettering over his doorway again.

"Well, well, well. I wonder how my name got there. Issi Noho. Mm . . ." he said thoughtfully, "Issi Noho. I like it. I think it suits me."

Issi stooped extra low to make sure he didn't hit his head on the top of the doorway. He slumped into the dry bracken he had collected for his bed, and he lay back. His comfortable roundness fitted exactly into the dent in the bracken. He clasped his big paws over his tummy, checked to make sure that his leather pouch was safe, and closed his eyes. His head still ached a tiny bit, but his mouth was full of the taste of licorice.

"Mm . . . different from bamboo shoots," he murmured to himself, "but equally delicious, equally delicious."

And this was the last thought he remembered thinking before falling into a peaceful and very contented snooze.

Chapter 2

A most bedraggled and soggy panda

Teatime at the Martins' was an abnormally quiet affair. Andrew struggled to cut up his beans on toast, trying not to spill too many beans on the clean tablecloth, but it was difficult because his thoughts were buzzing about his new friend Issi and not about his beans.

Sally sipped her milk and said nothing. She did so want to tell her mother about Issi, but she and Andrew had sworn each other to secrecy.

The only noise came from Claire, their baby sister, who punctuated every mouthful of fish fingers with her usual spoon-banging exercises on her plastic tray.

"Are you sure you feel all right, Andrew?" asked his mother.

"Of course I feel all right, Mum! Why?"

"Well, you're so quiet, dear," said his mother.

"But you're always telling me to be quiet at meals," retorted Andrew, and to this his mother could not reply for indeed she usually had to tell him so many times to speak less and eat more that she had vowed on more than one occasion to have her comment put on tape and so save her own voice.

Tea speeded on its way. Without the chat which usually accompanied each mouthful Andrew and Sally downed their food in half the time.

"Please may we leave the table?" asked Sally.

"Not until Claire has finished her tea," replied her mother.

"But she'll take ages," Andrew complained.

"It always pays to sit a while after your meal and digest it properly," said his mother firmly.

Andrew and Sally fidgeted, and Andrew, who hated wasting a moment, decided that if he had to continue sitting at the meal table he might as well eat some more.

"May I have another piece of cake?"

"There's a word missing," said his mother.

"Please."

"Very well – but chew it."

Andrew wondered how you could eat cake without chewing it, but decided not to give his mother cause for complaint by voicing his thoughts.

"*Oh no!*" cried Sally. "It's raining."

"Well, you've both had a good day out in the fresh air; it won't hurt you to stay in this evening. It would be rather nice if you played with Claire before she goes to bed," suggested their mother.

"But we want to go out!" spluttered Andrew through his Swiss Roll.

"Don't speak with your mouth full," said his mother sternly. "You're growing into a very selfish boy. I am not letting you get soaked tonight. I don't want you ill in bed with a cold. We've all got to be fit for our holiday next week. Your father has worked hard all year for it, and he needs a rest. Now let's hear no more about going out again tonight."

"But Mum . . ."

"Any more and you'll go straight to bed."

Andrew cast a despairing glance at the weather. It was raining harder than ever.

"He'll get soaked," said Sally absent-mindedly, thinking of Issi.

"Who'll get soaked?" asked her mother.

"Oh, er – Andrew. He'll get soaked if he goes out in this," Sally gabbled.

Andrew was furious. He felt his silly sister had really spoilt his chance of going out now, and he sent a well-aimed kick under the table which found its mark.

"Ouch!" cried Sally.

"That does it," said his mother firmly. "Go straight up to your room and don't dare to come out until I tell you."

Andrew jumped up from the table in a temper, sending his chair flying. It crashed

into the piano, leaving a large scratch on the front of the keyboard. Claire began to cry.

Andrew stamped upstairs, tears welling in his eyes. Everything had happened so quickly. One minute all had been quiet and perfect and the next his whole world had crumbled. He flung himself on his bed, muttering about the injustice of grown-ups, but finally he allowed his loss of pride at being sent to his room in front of his sisters, and the overwhelming unfairness of the whole episode, to flood out in heart-rending sobs. After a few moments he felt better.

Sally peeped round his door.

"What are we going to do?" she asked helplessly. "We promised to go back to see Issi with some more licorice. He'll think we're not interested in him if we don't go. We're the only friends he's got, and now he'll never trust us again."

"We're going back to see him," said Andrew resolutely. "That packing case will never stand up to rain like this. It's bucketing down now and he's going to need us."

"But how can we go back? You heard

what Mummy said. She'll never let us out now."

"Then we'll just have to go out without her knowing," said Andrew, and instructing his sister to shut the bedroom door he began to outline a plan.

Mrs Martin was most surprised half an hour later to find Andrew in his pyjamas and in bed.

"Now don't be silly, you can come down now. It's all over and done with and I shan't tell your father."

"I'm feeling rather tired, Mum, so I thought I'd go to bed early," said Andrew, giving as authentic a yawn as he possibly could. "And I do so want to be fit for our holiday."

"I knew there was something the matter," said his mother, sitting on the edge of the bed. "It's not like my boy to sit through tea saying nothing and then lose his temper so quickly. You get a good night's rest. I'll send Daddy up to kiss you good night when he comes in."

She leant forward and gently kissed him on his forehead. Andrew threw his arms round his mum's neck and gave her a hug. He hated deceiving her like this.

He'd never done it before. But he knew that the first thing a grown-up would do on hearing about Issi would be to ring for the police, and that would mean Issi being caught, crated up and carted off to the nearest zoo, or back to China. No – for Issi's sake his discovery had to remain a secret.

"Good night, Mum," said Andrew, and he turned over as if to go to sleep.

When Mrs Martin found Sally in bed as well she didn't know what to think. Sally told her the same tale, and her mother, thinking of all the work she had to do to prepare for the family's holiday, decided not to question any further but to use her time profitably to finish the ironing.

At last the house was quiet. Daddy had come home and, although surprised to find Andrew and Sally in bed and supposedly asleep, he accepted his wife's explanation. The evening dragged on endlessly as the children strove to keep awake. At long last the familiar routine of shutting windows, locking doors and shutting the boiler off commenced, and finally the bathroom light clicked off following the last gurgle of toothpaste which whirled down the plug hole. All was quiet.

Andrew and Sally were bursting with excitement, but they had vowed not to leave their rooms until at least half an hour after the final click of the bathroom light. When at last Andrew gently opened his door his father's snores sounded very reassuring.

He already had his dressing-gown on and had been clutching his pocket torch for so long it felt quite hot. He padded softly over the landing to Sally's door, gently opened it and gave two flashes on his torch. Sally had been waiting for the signal and was by his side almost at once. She followed her brother quietly downstairs. They stepped over the top step which squeaked and over the sixth which squeaked, and Andrew stepped over the first step on the bend towards the bottom of the staircase. Sally forgot and stepped on it. The creak that resounded through the stillness made both children freeze in their tracks, and they stood for what seemed an age before venturing on to the cloakroom cupboard. They fished out their wellington boots from the jumble of footwear and pulled on the rustling mackintoshes over their dressing-gowns. Then as quietly as they could they made for the front door.

"Hold it," whispered Andrew, "I've forgotten the licorice."

He moved silently into the kitchen and opened the sweet drawer. After rummaging a moment he found three licorice shoelaces and stuffed them in his pocket. He joined his sister in the hallway and she opened the door. They stepped outside.

Andrew gently closed the door behind them. It clicked shut.

It was still pouring with rain, and although it was quite warm both children shivered, mainly from excitement, as they walked deliberately and as quietly as they possibly could up the scrunchy gravel path to the gate. It was dark. The street lamps in Juniper Avenue had gone out and the only light they had was from Andrew's torch.

They quickened their steps, turning right at the end of their lane, second left into Coppins Avenue and first right into Coppins Close. Coppins Wood loomed up before them.

Sally stopped.

"I'm . . . I'm not sure this is such a good

idea after all," she whispered.

"Oh, you're scared. I knew you'd be scared," said Andrew disgustedly. Truth to tell he was feeling scared himself, but this was not the time to give in to such feelings.

"No I'm not!" said Sally. "I just feel we're being deceitful to Mummy and Daddy." She wasn't going to let her brother think she was frightened.

The rain seemed determined to find its way underneath their mackintosh collars and down their necks, and as they moved further into the wood it began to attack them from the other end as well. The soaked undergrowth reached above their wellingtons and dampened their night clothes.

Deeper and deeper into the woods they went as Andrew tried to remember the exact spot where Issi lived.

"It's just beyond those brambles over there," he murmured to Sally, "in the middle of that thicket."

Sally suddenly felt very strange and frightened. Coppins Wood, which by day was welcoming and friendly, was a very scary place in the dead of night and, well, she'd only met Issi once. Perhaps pandas are fierce if you disturb them at night.

Andrew forced his way onwards. His sudden cry brought Sally quickly to his side. She peered through the darkness into the clearing to discover the cause of her brother's dismay.

Sure enough it was the right place, but neither of them was prepared for the sight that met their eyes. There in the middle of the clearing where Issi's house had stood only a few hours before was a heap of shattered splintered wood and tangled foliage.

"There's been an accident! Issi may be under this mess! Perhaps he's hurt!"

They both ran forward and began feverishly clawing pieces of timber away from the wreckage, but after a minute or two it became obvious that Issi was not there. They stopped and looked at each other. After their energetic effort everything now seemed extra still and uncanny. The silence was broken only by the rain as it cascaded over the foliage and pattered on to their mackintoshes. They felt strange and uneasy.

"Where can he be?" whispered Sally.

"I don't know," whispered Andrew.

Suddenly the natural sounds of the woodland were shattered by an almighty sneeze. Andrew and Sally were rooted to the spots on which they stood. Their blood froze. Neither moved. Neither breathed. There was a clumsy rustling in the thicket over to the right. Andrew swung the beam of his torch in the direction of the noise, and there, staggering into the shaft of light, was the most bedraggled and soggy creature they had ever set eyes upon.

Chapter 3

Blinding flashes and puffs of green smoke

Sally was not at all sure that they ought to have brought Issi back to their house. At least she had stopped Andrew taking him into the house itself, but as the rainwater tumbled from their mackintoshes on to the thick carpet of their dad's new car she was not convinced of their wisdom in selecting the car as a good place to have a talk. However, the fact was that Issi's house was smashed. Issi had no home. It was pouring with rain and they were all getting wetter and wetter out in the woods, while the battery in Andrew's torch was so flat that the light from it barely glowed. To make for home seemed the obvious decision.

"I don't understand the bit about the magic going wrong," Andrew was saying.

"It always goes wrong," said Issi, sadly, chewing on the licorice shoelace that Andrew had provided.

"But it didn't all go wrong, did it?"

said Sally. "Because you actually managed to get your house up into the branches of the tree. It was just that the branches gave way under the weight and it fell to the ground and smashed."

Issi had already explained to them how his bed of bracken gradually lost its softness and cosiness and became damp, then wet and then distinctly soggy. He decided to magic his house up into the branches of a near-by tree where the rising damp could not reach him. Andrew and Sally were most intrigued by this mention of magic. They wondered if it had anything to do with the mysterious flash and puff of green smoke he'd mentioned earlier.

"But how did you magic your house up into the tree? What did you do?" Andrew persisted.

Issi tugged at the leather pouch which hung on the cord round his neck and shook out several tiny cards. On each card was a drawing of a large square divided into nine smaller squares, and in every square except one was a number.

"My father gave me these," he said, a certain pride creeping into his voice. "They have been handed down in my family

from generation to generation. They were first given to an ancestor of mine who was privileged to be a mascot to one of the greatest Chinese Emperors. The trouble is they're a bit unreliable."

"But what are they? How do you make them work?" asked Sally.

"They're magic squares," said Issi, "and if you want to make some magic you have to compose a little rhyme saying what you want to happen. Then you fill in the missing number on the magic square and your wish comes true. Except," he added in a rather disappointed sort of voice, "in my case it doesn't. The trouble is I'm not very good at making rhymes and I'm not very good at arithmetic."

"How are you supposed to work out the missing number?" asked Sally, who was very good at arithmetic.

"I'll show you," said Issi. "This is the card I used to magic my house into the tree." The children studied the card by the glow from the interior car light.

The middle number was obviously the one that Issi had filled in. It wasn't as neat as the others.

"Each line across, each line down, and each line from corner to corner is supposed to add up to the same total," explained Issi. "The middle square was empty, and I had to fill in the right number. The trouble is I can't add up very well, so I just guess."

Sally was quickly adding up the top line.

"Eight, plus one, plus six makes fifteen," she said.

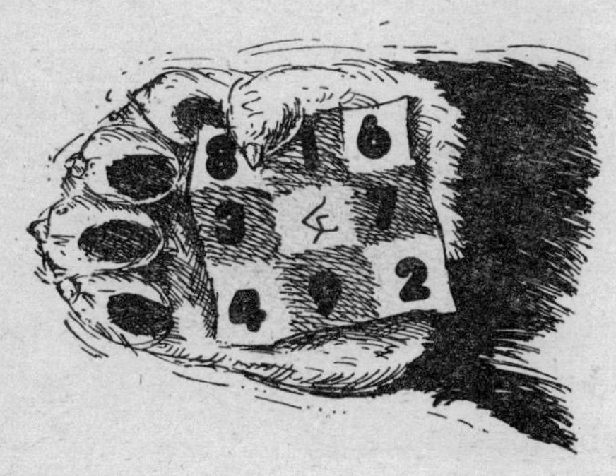

Then she added up the bottom line across.

"Four, plus nine, plus two makes fifteen."

Next she added up the first line down, eight, plus three, plus four, and then the third line down, six, plus seven, plus two. They all added up to fifteen.

"That means you need a number in the middle which makes all the other lines add up to fifteen," she said.

"Five," said Andrew.

Sally thought for a moment.

"I tell you it's five," said Andrew.

"Andrew's right, you should have put five in the middle square, not four," said Sally. "Then every line adds up to fifteen no matter which way you count them. I say – how clever!"

"Mm," said Issi. "I wasn't far out with four, was I?" He was rather pleased with his guesswork.

"You guessed near enough to make the magic work a little but not completely," said Sally. "Obviously four was near enough to get your house up into the tree, but if you want things to work out and stay as you want them, you have to be absolutely accurate."

"What was the rhyme you made up?" asked Andrew.

"Ah yes, I was rather proud of my rhyme," said Issi. "It went like this." He cleared his throat.

"I'm getting wet as wet can be,
Please put my house up in that tree."

Issi was particularly proud of having remembered the word "please".

"And what happened exactly?" asked Sally.

"I wrote four in the magic square. There was a blinding flash and a puff of green smoke and my house disappeared from the ground. I looked up and there it was. It was balanced rather precariously on a branch of the tree, but at least the tricky bit was done. I began to climb the tree to make it more secure, and I was half-way up the trunk when . . ." He broke off as the painful memory flooded back to him.

"When what?" urged Andrew.

"When it happened," said Issi simply. "There was a creaking sort of noise." He paused.

"Yes?"

"And a scraping sort of noise, and a loud swishing sort of noise and . . ."

The children waited patiently for Issi to tell the disastrous details.

"I looked down," he continued, "and there was my beautiful house, except that it wasn't beautiful any longer. It was just a heap of broken wood. Even my name over the door was broken into three pieces."

Sally thought she detected a tear in Issi's eye as he finished the sad tale, particularly when he mentioned the bit about his name, but he was so wet anyway that it could have been just rainwater.

The children suddenly knew they had been right to come. Poor Issi was certainly a sorry sight, and if anyone ever needed a friend it was Issi at that very moment. However, they really had got themselves into a bit of a mess. They were soaked to the skin and the carpet of their father's new car was now well and truly spongy with water.

"What on earth are we going to do now?" asked Sally.

"We must go inside the house and dry off," said Andrew firmly.

"But what about Issi?"

"He must come too," said Andrew. "We can't leave him out in the rain with no home to go to, now can we? We'll just have to hide him in the spare bedroom or something, until we can think of what to do for the best."

Sally hoped that the "or something" would be a better idea than hiding Issi in the spare bedroom, but as she couldn't think of an alternative the three of them crept out of the car and along the path towards the house.

Sally moved stealthily up to the front door and pushed it. Nothing happened. She pushed harder. The door refused to budge.

"You did put the door on the catch when we came out, didn't you?" she whispered.

"No," said Andrew, "I thought you did!"

"You goof," said Sally crossly. "We've locked ourselves out!"

For several seconds they stood still, at a loss to know what to do. Then Andrew decided that Issi should go back into the garage while he walked round the house one way and Sally the other looking for a window that might have been left ajar, although knowing his father's extreme care in locking up it was rather a forlorn hope.

Sure enough everywhere was securely

locked and within three minutes the children had rejoined Issi in the garage. All they had collected for their pains was more rainwater and lots of mud on their boots.

"I know," cried Sally. "Issi's magic squares. We'll use those."

"Do you think your magic squares could get us into the house?" asked Andrew.

"Well," said Issi doubtfully, "they might."

"I can do the arithmetic," said Sally.

"And I can make up the rhyme," added Andrew.

But Issi slowly shook his head.

"No," he said.

"No?"

"No," repeated Issi. "I'm afraid the magic squares only work for me. Well," he corrected himself, "only almost work for me. You see they have been handed down to me and they only work for the person to whom they have been given. Otherwise I would be only too grateful for a little help."

"Oh," said Sally.

"Well, I think it's still worth a try," said Andrew. "Anything would be better than waking up Mum or Dad or breaking a window to get in."

Sally wasn't so sure. She couldn't forget the sad result of Issi's attempt to magic his house into a tree. But Issi was already fumbling with his magic cards. He selected one which he placed on the bonnet of the car. Then he pulled the little pencil from his pouch and began studying intently the card he had chosen.

"Can't we help, just a little?" pleaded Sally.

"I'm afraid not," said Issi. "Any help from anyone will immediately cancel all the magic power in the card."

"Well, remember we want to get inside our house, preferably up in my bedroom," Andrew reminded him, and then he added, "without a sound."

"Oh dear, this is most difficult," said

Issi, "you're making me quite nervous."

His hand hovered over the empty square on the card.

Sally and Andrew had already worked out what the middle number should be if all the lines were to add up to the same amount.

"Can't we give you just the tiniest clue?" begged Andrew.

"No. Now please stop worrying. I'm sure I can guess near enough to get us all quite close to your bedroom," Issi assured them.

"But that's not good enough," said Andrew. "We might all land up at the foot of Mum and Dad's bed!"

"Or on the roof!" Sally wailed.

Issi threw down his pencil.

"Do you want me to help you or not?" He sounded a little impatient. He didn't often lose his temper, but the strain of trying to work out the mathematical problem and make up a rhyme, while the children breathed anxiously down his neck, was beginning to make him feel most uncomfortable.

The children began to shiver with the dampness and the chill night air. They felt tired and their tiredness made them anxious.

"Go on Issi," said Sally encouragingly. "We know you can do it."

All was very quiet for what seemed an age although it could only have been about a minute. Issi kept muttering to himself.

"I'm ready," he announced suddenly.

The children quietly crossed their fingers for luck. They were willing Issi to write the figure six in the centre square.

"I'm going to say the rhyme – now," said Issi.

"Into Andrew's bedroom whisk us away,
Quietly and secretly – don't delay."

On the word "delay" Issi poised his pencil over the magic square. The children held their breath. Then to their horror they saw Issi write slowly and deliberately the figure seven in the middle square.

"No!"

"But —"

Their protests were cut short by a blinding flash and a puff of green smoke, and all at once they landed in a jumbled heap on the floor.

For a moment they lay quite still.

"Are you all right?" whispered Andrew.

"Yes," Issi and Sally whispered back.

They began to untangle their limbs and squirm into crouched sitting positions. Everywhere was total darkness. Not a glimmer of light helped their straining eyes.

"It worked, it worked," whispered Issi excitedly.

"It worked all right," whispered Andrew. "The only problem is you were one out in the answer you put in your magic square. You've got us into the house all right, but whereabouts in the house? It's certainly not my bedroom."

Chapter 4

Enough magic for one night

"It's best if you both keep quite still while I interrogate our position," said Andrew.

"You mean investigate. Interrogate means to ask questions," said Sally.

"If you know what I mean why must you always show off? You make mistakes too," Andrew said crossly.

"Sorry. I was only trying to help."

"Well, you can help by keeping perfectly still while I look around," said Andrew, not wishing to attempt the word "investigate" again.

The battery in his torch had revived a little and when he switched it on the glow seemed quite bright in contrast to the pitch blackness.

He carefully edged forward, trying to identify something which would give a clue as to their whereabouts. Slowly he swung the dull beam from his torch round the room. The battery was fading quickly but before the light failed completely Andrew had seen enough; a pile of suitcases, an old standard lamp, cardboard boxes, an ancient sewing-machine, a tailor's dummy, a water tank and several piles of books. These things revealed quite clearly where they were. They were in the loft.

"But we can't get out," breathed Sally. "The bolt is on the underside of the trap-door."

"It's not a very strong bolt, though," said Andrew. "If we can lever the extensive ladder up slightly . . ."

"Extending ladder," said Sally before she could stop herself.

"Look – if you can't think of any ideas of your own stop finding fault with my vocabulary," Andrew retorted. He was getting angry with his sister. She hadn't come up with any bright ideas and seemed quite happy to play second fiddle except when it came to silly words, and even the most correctly spoken English wasn't going to get them out of their present trouble.

"As I was saying, if we can gently lever up the 'extending'," he looked pointedly at Sally, "ladder, I think the bolt will snap off. It shouldn't make much noise and

I'm blowed if I'm going to sit up here for the rest of the night."

"Perhaps," whispered Issi, "I could use another magic card to get us out of the loft."

"No thank you," said Andrew. "Apart from the fact that we can't see anything I think you've done enough magic for one night."

He spoke abruptly and Issi thought a little ungratefully, but then they were all very tired, and what had started out as an exciting adventure was beginning to turn into a nightmare.

"Now mind where you put your feet," warned Sally, "the loft isn't completely boarded in. If we slip off the joists our feet will go right through the ceiling."

To everyone's relief Andrew's plan worked like a charm. They found the extending ladder without putting their feet through the ceiling. They gingerly levered it up, applying pressure on the trap-door. There was a gentle click as the screws on the bolt gave way, and a soft thud as the bolt fell on to the landing carpet. The trap-door slowly opened as Andrew continued to lift the end of the ladder which was securely bolted to the upper side of it.

A shaft of light from the landing pierced the darkness of the loft. The Martins always left the landing light on all night and never had the children found it so comforting as at this moment.

Quickly Andrew lowered the ladder. Fortunately it was well oiled and slid smoothly, coming to rest gently on the generous pile of the landing carpet.

"Now you stay here until morning," said Andrew to Issi. "Here's all the licorice I have," he added, handing Issi the two licorice shoelaces left in his pocket. "You'll be quite comfy and warm and we'll bring you some breakfast as soon as Mum goes shopping in the morning. We can discuss further plans then."

Sally took a deep breath of relief. Of course, Issi could stay in the loft. This was the "or something" she had hoped for when Andrew had suggested putting Issi in the spare bedroom "or something". The loft was a much safer place than the spare bedroom.

"I'm sorry to put you to all this trouble," said Issi. "I really am most grateful. You're real friends."

Suddenly it all seemed worth while to Andrew and Sally. Suddenly it looked as if everything was going to be all right after all. Suddenly they could go back to bed safely, having saved their new friend from a most uncomfortable situation. Suddenly they could cope with everything once more, and they felt good.

"Now don't make a sound," whispered Andrew to Sally as she squeezed through the tiny trap-door, her foot groping for the top step. The ladder creaked alarmingly.

"I can't help it," mouthed Sally.

"Shh . . ."

"Shh . . ."

They held their breath and listened.

There was no movement from their parents' bedroom.

Andrew manœuvred himself through the narrow rectangular opening. The ladder creaked again, and he was glad when he reached the landing.

Andrew began to push the ladder back along its well-oiled runners. He knew that when it was pushed up there came a point when the weight of the ladder above the trap-door counterbalanced the rest, and it quietly lifted itself into the loft gently closing the trap-door behind it. But he hadn't the height to push it far enough.

"You'll have to lift me up," he whispered.

Andrew jumped. Sally clasped him in mid air for a split second. He flung a set of desperately outstretched fingers towards the bottom rung of the ladder. The ladder moved and then stuck. Andrew and Sally toppled on to the landing carpet in a jumble of slippery mackintosh and muffled grunting.

They lay quite still. Both were exhausted by their night's escapade and Andrew was at a loss to know how to push the ladder any further. But as luck would have it he had done enough. After a despairing pause the ladder slowly moved upwards of its own accord, gently closing the trap-door behind it. The children just had time to give a hasty wave to the two bright and thankful eyes that stared down at them from the loft before the trap-door clicked into position.

Andrew and Sally looked at each other and grinned. Andrew offered his hand to his sister and they gave each other an exaggerated and very meaningful hand-shake. They picked themselves up from the landing floor and crept quietly to their bedrooms.

Neither of them gave a thought to the trail of clues they had left behind them, each bearing witness to their night's adventure.

Chapter 5

Firmly and immovably stuck

Mr Martin rose sharply at seven o'clock as he always did on weekdays.

His first journey to the bathroom each morning was always taken in a twilight daze. He didn't really begin to wake up until he had splashed cold water four or five times into his face. So it was not surprising that his brain did not register the slight dampness his feet experienced as they padded over the landing carpet. It did register a slight pain as his toe stubbed against the bolt which had fallen from the trap-door, but he did not question it. He just stumbled mechanically onwards to the bathroom.

He emerged from the bathroom several minutes later very much more aware of what the day had to offer. This time the resounding clatter of the bolt as he accidentally kicked it down the stairs did register. He picked it up, looked up at the trap-door and shrugged his shoulders. He placed it carefully on the hall table, mentally earmarking yet another job to do at the weekend.

He opened the front door and leant outside to pick up the milk. He picked it up, closed the front door, then opened it again. Did his eyes deceive him so early in the morning or had he seen deep footprints in the flower beds disappearing round the side of the house?

He plugged the electric kettle in so that it could be boiling for the early morning cup of tea while he investigated the footprints further.

"Burglars!" he kept muttering to himself as he donned his overcoat and shoes. "We've had burglars in the night!"

He followed the footprints right round the house and checked on each window in turn. The burglars obviously couldn't get in, he thought with satisfaction.

Then he noticed the mud on the garden path trailing off towards the garage. The side door of the garage had been left open. He hurried up the path to the garage and peered inside. One of the front doors of his new car was open and the interior light still glowed. Not content with trying to break into his house, the burglar had obviously tried to steal his car.

He looked inside to make sure that everything was intact. He checked the glove compartment. His expensive polaroid sunglasses were still there. It didn't look as if they had taken anything.

Then he noticed a puddle on the rubber mat just underneath the brake and accelerator pedals. He felt the carpet in the front. It was soaking wet. He checked the back of the car. Everything seemed to be all right. The only strange thing was that the carpet was soaked just like the one in the front.

As he stared at it indignantly his thoughts were interrupted by the kettle whistling. He hurried back to the kitchen to make the tea. While the tea was left standing for the regulation three and a half minutes he phoned the police.

Andrew and Sally had to be wakened

that morning for breakfast, a most unusual occurrence. Usually they were tumbling round their father's feet in the kitchen begging for a slice of toast to tide them over until their mother had drunk her cup of tea in bed, put her face on in the bathroom and spent another ten minutes preparing their breakfast.

Mr Martin never ate breakfast. A cup of tea and a slice of toast spread generously with butter and marmalade was all he required before taking over the bathroom from his wife in order to wash and shave and get ready for work.

That morning Andrew and Sally were still half asleep as they trooped downstairs in answer to their mother's repeated calls. As they rounded the post at the bottom of the stairs they stopped abruptly.

There, on the hall table next to the bolt which had fallen from the trap-door into the loft, was a policeman's helmet.

"Now we're for it," breathed Andrew.

"Whatever happens we mustn't tell anyone about Issi," whispered Sally. "He trusts us and we mustn't betray him."

"Of course," said Andrew, and not knowing quite what to expect they entered the dining-room.

Claire was seated in her high chair banging a spoon on the plastic tray in front of her and calling for some more "gluk" which meant milk. Andrew could never understand why she couldn't say "milk" – it was much easier to say than "gluk". Claire's face showed signs of the egg and bacon she had been struggling to eat.

"Ah, there you are, my dears," said their mother. "Now there's no need to be alarmed but Daddy is in the sitting-room talking to a policeman. We think we had burglars last night, but they didn't get into the house so there's no need to worry."

The expression on the children's faces showed surprise and relief. Fortunately neither had to think of anything to say because their mother rattled on about the footmarks in the flower bed. She was interrupted by the sound of the sitting-room door opening, signifying an end of Mr Martin's interview with the policeman, and hurried into the hall to discover what had happened.

"I wish everyone was as careful as you when it comes to locking up their homes of a night," the constable was saying. "You'd be surprised how careless some people are. Invite 'em inside, some do, you know. Anyway, sir, I'll report this at the station, but I'm sure you've nothing to worry about. The only puzzling thing is the size of the footprints. Obviously made by very small boots – children's boots if you ask me. My guess is they were made by kids up to some prank or other."

The voices tailed away as Mr and Mrs Martin escorted the policeman off the premises.

"We must get our mackintoshes dried and back in the cloakroom before Mum notices anything," whispered Sally.

"And what about our boots?" said Andrew.

"Boots, boots, boots, boots," shouted Claire and banged some more with her spoon on the tray.

"What did you do about your wet pyjamas?" whispered Sally.

"I draped them over the hot-water tank in the airing cupboard and slept in my vest and pants," said Andrew. "What about your nightdress?"

"I put the radiator on in my room and dried it on that."

"We must get some food up to Issi as soon as possible," said Andrew.

"Boots, boots, boots, boots," screamed Claire excitedly.

"Yes, dear, we're going to Boots this morning and Sainsbury's," said their mother coming back to the dining-room.

"Good-bye – be good," called their father slotting his head round the dining-room door. "I must be off."

"Good-bye dear. Have a good day at the office," called their mother and blew him a kiss. "Say good-bye to Daddy, children."

"Good-bye."

"Good-bye."

"Boots, boots, boots," cried Claire.

Andrew and Sally ate their breakfast quickly and almost in silence as their mother cleaned up Claire and put her in her pushchair ready to go to the shops. As they finished there was a knock at the door. It was Neil wanting to know if the Martins could come out to play.

"You can play with Andrew and Sally as long as you all go outside, Neil," said Mrs Martin. "I don't want children fussing around me today. I've a lot to do to get ready for the holiday. You're to be out of this house by the time I get back." And so saying off she went with Claire.

"Where's Issi?" asked Neil.

"In the loft," answered Andrew. "Come on, let's see how he is, I'll tell you all about how he got there later."

"It would be easier if Issi came down for some breakfast," said Sally. "I'll get some food and put it on the small table in the playroom while you fetch him."

As Andrew and Neil ran up the stairs Andrew thought he heard a muffled sneeze coming from the loft. He lifted the broom with which he'd thoughtfully provided himself and nudged the trap-door ajar.

"Issi," he called.

This time there was an unmistakable sneeze from the loft and two watery eyes peered down through the opening.

"Issi," called Andrew again, "are you all right?"

"I think I'be got a cold id by dose," said Issi miserably.

"Oh poor old you," said Andrew sympathetically. "Never mind, you'll feel better when you've had a good breakfast. Mum and Dad are out so we thought you might like to come down and have something to eat. You'll have to lever the ladder up until it slides down far enough for me to reach it."

"All right," said Issi. He really did sound most sorry for himself.

Andrew reached up and grabbed the bottom rung of the ladder. He gently pulled it down until it rested on the carpet. "Come on down," he called.

Almost at once Issi's black furry legs appeared through the trap-door.

"That's it. Just take it easy," said Andrew.

Issi negotiated the top two steps steadily. Then he stopped. His right leg seemed to be groping for the third step.

"Come on," said Andrew a little impatiently.

"I can't cub od. I'be stuck," said Issi.

Now although Issi was not very tall, he was very round. In fact he was almost as round as he was tall and this was the problem. His ample bulk seemed to be filling every available space the narrow trap-door could offer.

"Push harder."

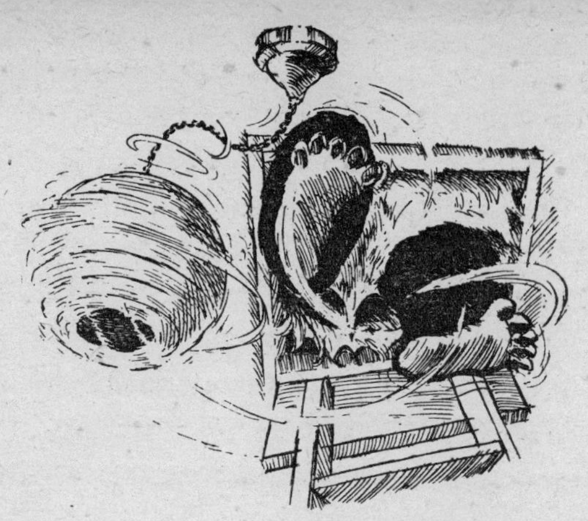

"I ab pushing harder," said Issi in some distress.

"All right, all right, now don't panic," said Andrew. "Climb back into the loft, Issi, and we'll have a think."

Issi's lower limbs struggled to gain a foothold so that he could thrust himself upwards. He was obviously having great difficulty.

"Hurry up," called Sally from the foot of the stairs. "We're wasting valuable time."

"Issi's stuck in the trap-door," Neil called back.

The news brought Sally hurtling up the stairs. "Don't just stand there – give him a push!" she cried.

"If we've got to push we may as well try and pull first. We haven't tried that," reasoned Andrew.

He climbed the ladder until he could gain a firm grip of Issi's legs and pulled with all his strength. Issi, who hadn't been informed of this change of plan and was still desperately trying to move upwards, suddenly found himself rapidly dropping. But alas, he only dropped three or four inches before his plump girth jammed itself tighter than ever in the hole.

Andrew immediately reversed the procedure and attempted to push Issi upwards again.

"Which way ab I supposed to be going?" called a puffed and puzzled Issi.

"Upwards," cried Andrew.

The next few moments were full of strenuous effort, pulling, pushing, tugging, heaving, puffing and panting. But the net result was a panda firmly and immovably stuck in the trap-door.

"Now we're in real trouble," panted Andrew.

Issi had given up the struggle. He just hung there and, every now and again, sneezed.

Chapter 6

Mrs Martin should have known better

Time ran out as time always does when one is in an impossible situation. The children, think as hard as they might, had not resolved the problem of the stuck panda by the time they saw their mother hurrying up the garden path home from the shops.

In that fleeting moment they decided upon the only option open to them. They would have to tell their mother the whole truth.

Mrs Martin's annoyance at finding the children still indoors changed to undisguised concern as Andrew approached with a very serious face to ask her if she would be kind enough to come into the lounge for a few minutes because he, Sally and Neil had something most important to tell her.

She sensed by his attitude that this was no ordinary "something" which she must be told with such solemnity. She put Claire in the pen in the playroom and then came into the lounge and sat down.

What she expected to hear we shall never know, but the story which burst and bubbled from the children took her completely by surprise. Out it all tumbled, the game of hide and seek, the strange meeting with a panda in Coppins Wood, the night's adventure . . .

"So they were *your* footprints on Daddy's flower beds!"

. . . the magic that was so unpredictable, and the panda who was now stuck half-way through the trap-door half in the loft and half hanging over the landing . . .

"Now, at this very minute, upstairs!" said their mother disbelievingly. She rose and marched straight to the foot of the stairs and looked up. The children followed close behind.

"Promise not to tell anyone," Andrew was saying desperately. But his mother wasn't listening, she was bent on seeing for herself the sight which would confirm the strange tale which had just been told her.

It was only as they tumbled up the stairs behind her that the children sensed that all was not as they had said it was.

Their mother had stopped and was staring up at the open trap-door. Indeed she was staring right through the trap-door since there was nothing to interrupt her gaze. Issi was nowhere to be seen.

"He must have dislocated himself after all," said Andrew, and squeezing past his mother he hurried up the ladder. Sally guessed that her brother had meant dislodged, but she was so concerned about Issi that she didn't bother to correct him.

"Issi, Issi," she called. "Are you all right?"

There was no answer. There was no movement, no sound, not the tiniest rustle.

"Issi," called Andrew, "come and have some breakfast, you must be very hungry."

"Don't be afraid, Issi," called Sally from the bottom of the ladder. "We've told Mummy about you and she's longing to meet you. Aren't you, Mummy?" she added, turning to her mother.

Her mother looked at her elder daughter very long and very hard.

"I am not sure what all this is about," she said slowly and firmly, "but I hope you find your magic panda, even if only to prove to me that my two eldest children are not after all quite dotty."

She didn't sound cross, her tone was more one of genuine bewilderment.

The scream that rent the house a moment later was all the more spine-chilling because of the silence it shattered, and because the children had never, ever known their own mother lose control of herself.

In fact Mrs Martin should have known better. Had she not after all just been talking with her children about a live panda? Had she not gone upstairs especially to see it half hanging out of the loft? Had she not been told at great length about its abilities to perform magical feats?

Perhaps it was all too much to absorb in

ten brief minutes. Sufficient to say that the sight of a large panda in Claire's playpen was just too much for her.

As her mother entered the playroom Claire had simply said "Bear bear", and playfully hit the panda over the head with a plastic rattle.

Her mother screamed – and what a scream! It wasn't the sort of scream that makes people run immediately to the aid of the screamer. It was the sort of scream that roots people to the spot while they decide in a moment of panic whether to run away from it instead of towards it. It was a fearful scream.

"Mummy!" shrieked Sally.

"It's Mum!" said Andrew aghast.

Their mother was slumped half in the hallway and half in the playroom. She had fainted.

While Sally fell to her knees to satisfy herself that her mother was not dead, Andrew thrust the door wide open to discover what unnerving spectacle had caused his mum to behave in such an "un-mumly" way.

Issi was playfully holding Claire aloft in his arms gently shaking her. Claire was giggling and trying to hit Issi anywhere she could reach with the plastic rattle.

"Look what I'be found," cried Issi happily.

"Now put my sister down, come out of that playpen and explain how you got there," said Andrew.

"Bagic," said Issi. "I had to fill the number on by bagic card in the dark too," he explained proudly. "I could hardly see a thing in that loft."

"Bear bear, bear bear," cried Claire. Never had she had such a wonderful toy to play with, one that actually played back, and was so warm and gentle and cuddly.

Issi sneezed.

"You've given my mum the fright of her life," said Andrew.

"I'be sorry," said Issi, "I realise I must hab scared the lady who cabe id, but I carried on playing with my dew friend so that she wouldn't be scared by the dreadful doise the lady made."

There must be few problems that a cup of tea cannot solve. The speed with which their mother overcame the shock and became once more the mum they'd known all these years was unbelievable.

In fact before the third sip of the cup of tea which Sally made them all, except Neil who preferred a Coke, Mrs Martin was more concerned about Issi's cold than anything else.

"You see," she explained, "we're all going on holiday next week and Mr Martin needs his holiday so much – well I'm sure you understand. If the children catch cold it . . . well I really don't know what we should do."

And it was this line of reasoning which lead to Issi finding himself warmly hot-water-bottled up in the guest bedroom within half an hour of that dreadful scream.

"We can't have you spreading your germs around downstairs," Mrs Martin reasoned as she tucked Issi in bed. "Now I'm afraid I'm not going to let you play with the children until you've got over your nasty cold. And I want you to eat and drink a lot. Feed a cold and starve a fever, that's how we treat 'em in this house. We'll have you fit in no time. Now what would you like to eat?"

Issi was indeed very hungry and the disappointment at finding there were no

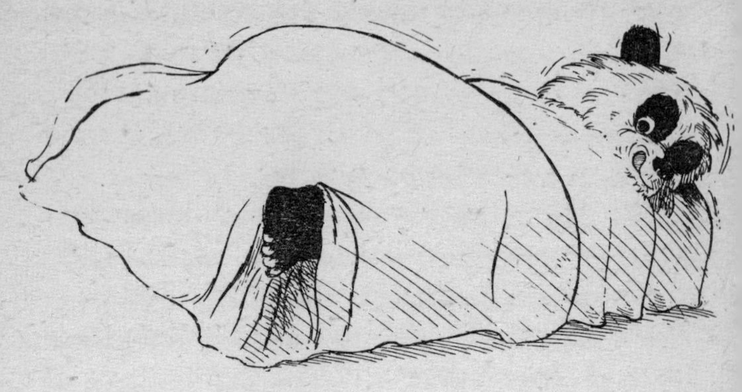

bamboo shoots in the Martins' larder soon faded as he found out that he liked cornflakes with milk and honey, fried bread, eggs and bacon, toast and marmalade and coffee.

"I like licorice too, you know," added Issi after he had told Mrs Martin how exciting and tasty he found all these new foods.

In some ways it had been a most satisfactory encounter. Mrs Martin had accepted Issi and Issi was certainly being well cared for. The fact that the children had to keep well out of Issi's way until his cold was better was a bit of a hardship, but one that could easily be borne. After all, it was only temporary and Andrew was already busily hunting for two old cocoa tins and a piece of string so that they could rig up their own private telephone service and communicate with their sick friend without catching his germs.

The big question mark which hung over the children's heads was, how would their father react to their new guest?

"Leave that one to me," said their mother confidently. "I've had years of experience in persuading your father to do the right thing."

Chapter 7

A rather sneezy sort of panda

If one searched for a word to sum up their father's attitude to his discovery that a real live panda was now occupying the guest bedroom, that word could only be "unreasonable". Or at least that's how it seemed to Andrew and Sally. In fact in spite of their mother's reassuring nods they felt rather let down. What about all these years of experience in persuading their father to do the right thing? The children could not see much evidence of them.

"I shall look extremely silly when I tell the police that the footprints round the house were made by my own children," their father was saying. "And heaven knows what they'll say when I tell them we have a panda in the house!"

"They'll be only too pleased to know it wasn't burglars," said their mother patiently. "And as for Issi, they need never be told about him."

"Never be told about him!" their father exploded. "In this country you need a licence for practically everything. You surely must need one for a panda. Of course we'll have to inform the police."

"You don't need a licence for a cat," said Andrew hotly. This was rather rude of him but he was angry at his father's lack of reason.

"Oh! I see, I suppose you're going to pass this – this very rare zoological specimen off as a domestic cat," retorted his father.

"Now I think this conversation is getting out of hand," said Mrs Martin firmly. "I think we should all go to bed and sleep on it. Then we can discuss the problem calmly," she emphasised the word "calmly", "in the morning."

"Sleep! Sleep!" roared Mr Martin. "You surely don't expect me to risk the lives of my family by allowing a live panda to stay under the same roof for a whole night!"

"My dear Charles," said Mrs Martin, "while your concern for your family is most touching I hardly think that a panda who can play as gently as a kitten with your youngest daughter and who, poor thing, has a shocking cold, is going to present a threat to anybody during the night. Why don't you come and meet him for yourself? Then you'll be in a better position to judge."

Mr Martin mounted the stairs with his wife. Andrew and Sally followed.

Mrs Martin knocked on Issi's door.

"Cub id," called Issi.

"I want you to meet my husband," said Mrs Martin. "Issi, this is Mr Martin. Mr – er – Charles dear – this is Issi."

Issi extended a paw from the bedclothes and before Mr Martin knew what he was doing he was shaking the paw in a very friendly manner.

"I'b so sorry to be causing your fabily so much trouble," said Issi. "I can't rebember ever habing a cold before. I feel a bit of a fraud tucked up in bed but I'd hate to pass it on to any of the fabily and spoil your holiday. You bust be looking forward to it so much."

"Well . . . er . . . yes, we are," said Mr Martin, taken aback by Issi's thoughtful and well-mannered approach.

"Now out you go, children," said their mother. "Daddy wants to have a chat with our new friend."

Andrew and Sally were hustled out of the room and their mother followed. "Now don't stay too long," she told her husband. "We don't want you catching cold, and Issi needs all the rest he can get."

"You're not leaving Daddy with Issi on his own are you?" whispered Sally in surprise.

"Just leave them to it," her mother said wisely. "There comes a time when you just have to leave things to sort themselves out – and this is one of those times."

"That panda mustn't be moved until he's quite better," said Mr Martin to his family, who had been waiting patiently for the outcome of his first encounter with Issi. "The poor thing is utterly exhausted. Heaven knows what he's been through. I think he's a little homesick as well, poor chap."

And with that he picked up the daily newspaper, filled his pipe and sat in his favourite armchair as though he was completely accustomed to coming home from work and finding a sick panda in the guest bedroom.

Andrew and Sally looked with utter

surprise at their mother, who winked at them knowingly.

"Time for bed," she said, as though the whole matter had been satisfactorily resolved and there was no more to be said.

"You know," said Andrew thoughtfully as he came out of the bathroom in his pyjamas, "Mum really has had years of experiments in handling Dad."

"I think the word you're looking for is 'experience', not 'experiments'," said Sally in a superior tone of voice as she swept past him to clean her teeth. Then, poking her head round the bathroom door, she added, "Women always do know how to handle their menfolk. That's something you'll learn as you grow older, little brother."

Later that evening Mr Martin phoned the police. He explained that the footprints in his herbaceous borders had been made by his own children and that as far as he was concerned the matter was closed.

He made no mention of Issi.

And so the days rolled by. Issi got well again and none of the Martins caught his cold.

Issi was soon like a member of the family. He slept in the guest bedroom, he ate in the dining-room, he played in the playroom and relaxed in the lounge. However, life was not without its problems. For instance, no one outside the Martin family, except Neil, knew of Issi's existence. Soon people would find out. And then there was the problem of the Martins' holiday. A dog can be housed in kennels, a cat can go to a cattery, but what does one do with a panda?

Fortunately, something happened to solve these problems.

Although Issi had recovered from his cold he remained a rather sneezy sort of panda. The billowy apricot-coloured eiderdown on his bed made him sneeze. He sneezed when the smell of breakfast fried bread made everyone else's mouth water. He sneezed when Mrs Martin did her vacuum cleaning, and when she shook her yellow duster out of the window. He sneezed at the smell of lunch-time vegetables cooking. He sneezed as the delicious aroma of smoked kipper fillets told everyone that tea was about to be served, and he sneezed when Mr Martin lit his pipe.

"I can't understand it," said Issi one day after a particularly violent fit of sneezing. "I never used to sneeze – ever."

"Ah, but then you've never lived indoors before, have you?" said Mr Martin. "Houses are very dusty places, you know, and . . ."

"Dusty! Dusty!" interrupted Mrs Martin indignantly. "I'll have you know that I never stop cleaning this house."

"Exactly my dear," said Mr Martin, "you prove the point I am making. If the house didn't get so dusty you wouldn't have to work so hard cleaning it. No – I think you're an outdoor sort of panda, Issi, and it's the indoor dusts and smells which make you sneeze so much."

"Oh Daddy, we can't send Issi back to Coppins Wood!" cried Sally.

"It wouldn't be fair," said Andrew hotly. "Issi's one of the family now."

"If you would let me explain," said Mr Martin. "I am not for one moment suggesting that Issi goes back to Coppins Wood. What I am about to suggest is that we build him his very own house at the bottom of our garden."

"Oh, that's a lovely idea!" cried Sally. "Would you like that Issi?"

"A house of my very own?" said Issi. "Oh . . . but . . . that would be wonderful but . . ."

"No 'buts' about it," said Mr Martin. "If you would like a house of your own in the fresh air, then you shall have one."

"When can we begin?" asked Andrew.

Mr Martin thoughtfully tapped the ash from his pipe into the ash tray.

"A . . . a . . . tishoo!" sneezed Issi.

"I think the sooner we begin the better," said Mr Martin.

And so when Neil called round to play he found Andrew and Sally drawing up detailed plans for Issi's new house, which they had decided to build in the big horse-chestnut tree at the bottom of the garden.

"You know," said Issi, "there's really no need to go to all this trouble. I can always magic a house for myself."

"Not until we've taught you how to add up the numbers on your magic cards," said Sally.

"If you're one number out, you know, your magic always goes wrong," said Andrew. "For the time being it will be much safer to construct a house by the normal methods."

So the children and Issi set to work in the garden shed.

Andrew and Neil did the skilful bits such as hammering the nails and screwing the screws while Issi did the fetching and carrying bits.

Sally's main task was to keep the workers supplied with a continual flow of orangeade and Coke.

All went well for a while. Then things began to go wrong. Andrew hit his thumb with the hammer and Sally had to bandage it.

Neil screwed his baggy jumper in between the two pieces of wood he was joining, and when he pulled it out and tore it, it was Sally who darned it for him.

And when Issi dropped a plank of wood on his paw it was Sally who soothed it by bathing it in a bowl of cool water.

The four of them took stock of the situation. There was still an awful lot to do.

"I still think it would be easier to magic a house," said Issi, who was quite worn out by all his fetching and carrying.

The children looked around at the terrible mess of bits and pieces that they were trying so hard to make into a house, and all at once the task seemed enormous.

"All right, Issi," said Sally, "have a go."

Issi took a magic card from the leather pouch hanging round his neck.

"I thought it might come to this," he said. "I've already worked out a little rhyme so there's no need to wait. I'll do it straight away."

"You're quite sure you've thought it all out?" asked Andrew anxiously, a little shocked by Issi's speed.

"Quite sure," said Issi confidently. "Now just make yourselves comfortable and watch."

The children tingled with excitement.

Issi spoke:

"Just like this shed please build for me
A house up in the horse-chestnut tree."

"Ugh!" muttered Sally, who didn't like Issi's poetry at all. But Issi didn't hear her. He was already filling a number in the magic square.

There was a blinding flash, and suddenly the garden shed was thick with billowy green smoke. The children started to cough. Tears streamed from their eyes as the smoke crept up their noses and down their throats.

As the smoke cleared Andrew pulled open the door, eager to see whether Issi's spell had worked. In that split second when he stepped outside Sally sensed that something was terribly wrong. She lunged and grabbed his jumper as Andrew with a bewildered gasp almost disappeared from view. His legs flailed in the air, desperately searching for the ground.

"Help me! Help me!" screamed Sally as the weight of her brother pulled her through the shed door. Neil grabbed her, and Issi grabbed Neil. Suddenly the terrifying exit from the shed was halted.

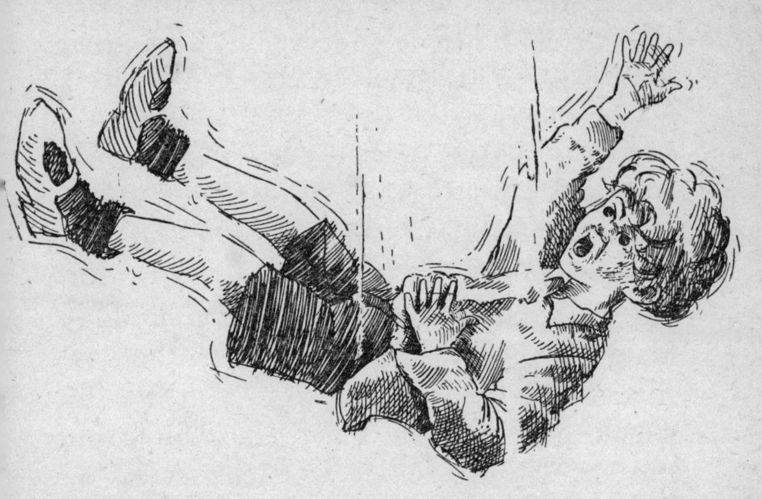

Andrew dangled in his jumper about twelve feet above the ground. Sally, half in and half out of the shed, clung on to her brother for dear life, while Neil and Issi prevented her from sliding out any further.

Far from building a house just like their father's shed high in the branches of the horse-chestnut tree, Issi's magic had transported their father's shed itself, complete with occupants, high into the branches.

Andrew's desperate cries brought his mother and father racing from the house. They stopped, staring in utter disbelief at the sight of the garden shed firmly implanted in the horse-chestnut tree, with their son hanging out of it and their daughter struggling to hold his ever-stretching jumper.

There was no time to fetch a ladder, no time to fetch a blanket. Mr Martin rushed forward. Andrew slid out through his jumper and landed in his father's outstretched arms. They landed in a jumbled heap on the grass, winded but otherwise none the worse.

A cup of tea in the Martin household was the surest cure of all problems. Half an hour after that terrifying episode the Martins were seated in their lounge with Neil and Issi, all sipping tea and fully recovered from the shock.

"Well, rather than go to the trouble of bringing my shed down from the tree," Mr Martin was saying, "I think the best solution is to leave it up there for Issi to live in while we build another shed for me on the ground."

"I can always magic a new shed for you," offered Issi.

"Issi dear," said Mrs Martin, "we very much appreciate your kind offer but you must admit that your magic really is most unreliable. In fact this last escapade could have ended with a very nasty accident."

"That's as may be," cut in Mr Martin as he noticed a rather sad expression in Issi's eyes, "but I've been thinking. It would be quite wrong for Issi simply to move out of the guest room and climb up into his new house without a celebration to mark the occasion. I think we ought to have a proper house-warming party for him. I'll organise a barbecue in the garden and we can take the opportunity to introduce Issi to all our neighbours."

And so for the first time in his life Issi was the chief guest at a party held in his honour.

Coloured fairy lights were festooned in the trees that night, and the delicious smell of barbecued sausages and hamburgers hung in the still evening air as Mr Martin, complete with chef's hat and apron, tossed, tweaked and nudged the sizzling meats until he judged them to be ready for the soft flour-dusted rolls. Lemonade and cider flowed like water. Music played and the early evening stars twinkled to its gay tunes.

It was Sally who detected that the guest of honour was not as happy as he should be.

"What's wrong, Issi?" she asked. "You've looked glummer and glummer all evening."

"Me glum?" said Issi forcing a very tiny laugh. "Why, I'm the happiest panda alive. I've got a new house and new friends, and everything that's happening tonight is because of me."

"Well, you may be the happiest panda alive," said Sally, "but I still think you're not as happy as you should be. Come on, tell me what's wrong. Don't you feel well?"

"I feel fine."

"Are you worried about us going on holiday and leaving you?"

"Of course not. You'll be coming back, won't you? No, I shall potter and get my house nicely sorted out while you're away."

"Then what is it?" persisted Sally. "Is there something about your house you don't like?"

Issi shuffled uncomfortably.

"Now come on, out with it."

"Oh, it's really nothing at all, honestly. It's just that you caught me as something rather sad was going through my mind, but it's nothing to worry about, I promise. If I told you you'd only laugh at me," said Issi.

"I'm not going to stop pestering you until you tell me what's on your mind, and I promise I shan't laugh," said Sally firmly.

"Well . . . I was just thinking, when you must have noticed the glum expression on my face, I was just thinking . . ."

"Yes?"

"It would be so nice to have my name over the front door of my new house. Just like I had it over my old one, do you remember?" Issi blurted this out a little sheepishly.

"Is that all?" cried Sally.

"I told you it was nothing really. It's just me being silly."

"Issi," said Sally, "we shall put that right immediately."

She ran off to Andrew and after a brief huddle Issi saw them both run off towards the garage. He lost track of them after that because Mr Martin had noticed him standing all on his own and decided that it was time for him to circulate and meet the residents from Juniper Avenue. He met

Mr and Mrs Kirby from number 43 and their two children Paul and Mark. He met Mr and Mrs Spencer from number 39 and their two children Debbie and Sarah. He met . . . he met . . . he met so many people, was asked so many questions, was shaken by the paw so many times, was laughed with and talked at so merrily and so much – he was happily confused and excitingly bewildered.

Suddenly Mr Martin called for everyone's attention.

"And now," he was saying, "and now for the formal part of the evening."

Everyone clapped and cheered.

"Issi, our new friend and neighbour, will now officially climb up the rope ladder and enter his new house."

Everyone clapped and cheered more loudly.

Even Issi found himself clapping and cheering. He wasn't sure what else to do.

Andrew stepped forward and took Issi by the paw. "Come on," he whispered, and led Issi over to the foot of the rope ladder that stretched upwards into the darkness of the tree to where his new house nestled securely in the branches.

"Now you have to climb up to your front door," instructed Andrew. "When you get there you'll see my pyjama cord hanging from the front door. When I give the signal you pull the cord. All right?"

Issi nodded.

As he began to climb the ladder someone chanted one, two, three, counting each rung as he stepped on to it. Soon everyone was chanting in chorus.

"Eleven, twelve, thirteen, fourteen. Hooray!"

Issi clambered on to the tiny platform outside his new front door. He looked down at all the upturned cheering faces. Andrew shouted, "Now Issi – now!" and Issi turned to find the cord which Andrew said would be there. He tugged it, and all at once a gaily coloured piece of curtain material fell from over the door. There, underneath, revealed by the gay fairy lights was a plaque. And on the plaque was written in round golden letters, "ISSI NOHO LIVES HERE."

Issi's happiness was complete.

Chapter 8

Now you see it, now you don't

Issi couldn't put a name to the deep feeling he had for the Martins, but in fact it was gratitude.

He was grateful for the way Andrew and Sally had befriended him. He was grateful for the way their parents had accepted him as one of the family. He was grateful for his new house. And he was grateful for the vast store of foodstuffs with which Mrs Martin had filled his larder before going off on holiday.

As always a deep feeling of gratitude is accompanied by a deep feeling of wanting to repay in some way the kindness of others.

The Martins had gone on their annual holiday for two weeks, and the one thing above all others which stuck in Issi's mind was something he overheard Mrs Martin say just before she left. It was something which hadn't been meant for his ears at all.

"What with one thing and another," Mrs

Martin had said, "I just haven't had time to give the house a really good tidy up and clean out."

"Never mind, my dear," her husband had replied philosophically, "it will still be here when you come back."

"That's just it," said Mrs Martin. "I do so like to come back to a house that's been well cleaned out. I shall have to leave it in such a mess this year. Oh dear."

Issi knew that his unscheduled arrival at the Martins' was the "one thing and another" she meant, and he felt unhappy to think that he was the reason for the house not looking spick and span.

He was determined to put the matter right and to repay the debt he felt he owed. He began to think what he might do.

It came to him in a flash, like most things do. It's truly amazing how you can sit for hours on end pondering a problem, then suddenly – just when you're not thinking about it at all – in fact just when you're thinking how very delicious raspberry jam sandwiches can be – suddenly at that very moment you feel inspired.

Issi forgot about the delicious tea he was enjoying.

"Why, of course!" he said to himself, "I shall magic their house tidy for them."

He knew his magic didn't always work properly, but the house was locked, and it was only by magic that he could clean it.

"Anyway," he said to convince himself, "my magic always works well enough to get me out of trouble, so even if the house is only half cleaned out it will be something. Better than none of it being cleaned out at all, with poor Mrs Martin having to work so hard to clean it out that she needs another holiday to get over it."

Issi was so carried away by his plan that he almost forgot to finish his raspberry jam sandwich. Fortunately, a slight rumble in his tummy indicated a small space still to be filled, and he estimated that the amount of bread and jam remaining on his plate was just the right amount to fill the rumbly space.

Issi finished his tea. He felt physically and mentally well satisfied.

Before actually carrying out his magic he decided to practise his arithmetic, and for several days he applied himself diligently to adding up sums of all kinds.

While Issi was to be congratulated for

not sparing any effort at all in using his brain until it ached, he could be faulted, if one wished to be unkind, for the complete waste of time it all was since he had not taken the precaution of asking someone to check his arithmetic. The result was that he had no idea whether he was getting better at sums, or worse, or, indeed, simply staying as he was – which was not very good. But one cannot be unkind when someone is working so hard with such good intentions.

Truth to tell the more Issi worked at his arithmetic, the more he grew nervous about its possible outcome, until at last the day of the Martins' return dawned.

"Well," said Issi, "it's now or never. If I don't do it today it will be too late."

And so saying he opened his leather pouch and drew out a magic card. It looked like this:

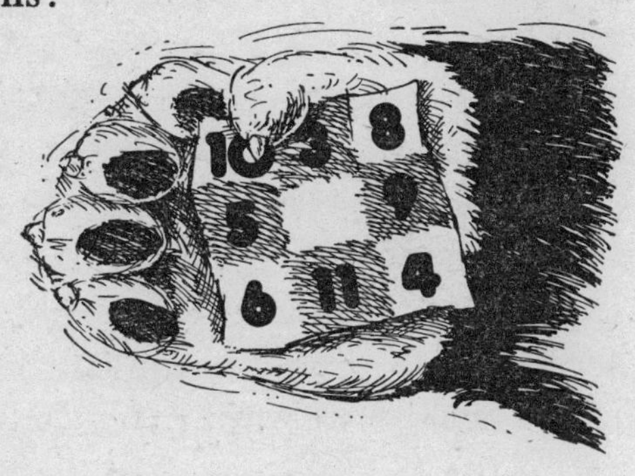

He thought of the number on which he was going to pin his faith. There was then nothing left to do but press right on with the magic spell itself.

He had already made up a rhyme, and he recited it solemnly and slowly.

"O magic card be free from doubt,
Please clean the Martins' house right out."

Then he took hold of his pencil and wrote the figure seven in the middle square of his magic card.

Before he began the spell he positioned himself by his front door so that the Martins' house was in full view. And now, as soon as he had filled the number in the square, he looked up expectantly.

There was a blinding flash and an enormous puff of green smoke which completely enveloped the Martins' house. And then there was nothing – literally nothing.

As the green smoke thinned, scattered by the early morning breeze, there was not the slightest, tiniest, minutest trace of number 41 Juniper Avenue. The plot of land where the Martins' house had stood was quite distinctly marked out by its concrete footings, but the actual residence itself had completely disappeared.

It is difficult to know who was the more dumbfounded, Mr Birkenshaw the milkman who was just about to place four pints of milk on the doorstep when the doorstep vanished, or Issi, who at least was expecting something to happen.

Mr Birkenshaw left the four pints of milk where the doorstep should have been and backed down the path to the front gate which he was relieved to find still existed. Not for one second could he take his eyes off the Martins' house, or rather the gaping nothingness which had now replaced the house. He stood at the gate, dazed, as you do when something happens and all your senses assure you that it hasn't happened because it just can't happen.

"I'll never touch another drop as long as I live," he muttered to himself, recalling the darts match at the Keg and Noggin on the previous night. "So help me I'll never touch another drop."

And with that he ran to his milk float, jumped in, and drove just as quickly as a milk float can be driven to the police station.

Issi rubbed his eyes, looked, and rubbed his eyes some more. But no amount of rubbing changed the view from his front door. The Martins' house had utterly completely, and without trace – vanished.

Chapter 9

"I'd like to report a missing house!"

Mr Birkenshaw was well known to the police. Not because he was a criminal but because, being a milkman, he often witnessed things which were of interest to the police. He witnessed the odd accident. He found the odd missing cat or tortoise. And he was usually the first to discover the odd old person in distress and in need of help.

"G-good morning, Mr Birkenshaw," said Constable Pinks.

"Good morning, Mr Pinks," said Mr Birkenshaw shakily.

"And to what do we owe the honour of your visit today?" asked Constable Pinks.

"I want to report . . . ," and here Mr Birkenshaw paused. "I want to report a . . . er . . . a missing house."

"I really don't know what we'd do without you and your keen eyes roving the neighbourhood," said Constable Pinks, taking down the blue report book. "Honestly – some people would lose their own head if it wasn't fixed on. Now what was it again you wish to report?"

"A missing house," repeated Mr Birkenshaw slowly and firmly.

Constable Pinks chuckled. "That's a good one," he said. "Shouldn't give us much trouble finding that, should it?"

"I'm afraid it's true," said Mr Birkenshaw, "I only wish it was a joke, but number 41 Juniper Avenue has completely disappeared."

The tone of the milkman's voice and the serious expression on his face took the smile off the constable's face. "Come, come now Mr Birkenshaw, it's not April Fool's day you know," he said, trying to humour his visitor.

"I wish it were," said Mr Birkenshaw, "but as true as I'm standing here I was just about to deliver four pints of milk on the doorstep when it vanished."

"Ah!" said the constable, detecting a glimmer of sense. "I see – the doorstep subsided, did it? Disappeared beneath the ground. Funnily enough we had a case of a subsiding doorstep only last year. The gas men had been laying new pipes in Thornden Road, didn't fill in the holes properly they didn't, and before we knew where we were we had two doorsteps and a portico subside – caved right in they did."

But Mr Birkenshaw persisted with his unlikely tale of the vanishing house until Constable Pinks made a decision.

"Right," he said. "It's not that I don't believe you, you understand, but before I record such an important piece of information in the book I think I'd better come and investigate it for myself. Can't be too careful with . . . er . . . missing houses," he said. He felt he had to humour Mr Birkenshaw. All the while he spoke he searched the milkman's face for a sign that it was after all some sort of practical joke. But the ashen face of the milkman gave no such sign.

"Well, let's go then, shall we?" said the constable, picking up his helmet. "How about you giving me a lift in the milk float?" And he led the milkman out of the police station.

Meanwhile Issi had not remained idle. First of all he had investigated the site where the Martins' house had stood to make sure that he wasn't seeing things, or wasn't not seeing things, as the case was. Then he hurried back to his little home in the tree and pulled a batch of magic cards from the pouch round his neck. He studied each one in turn but they all seemed equally difficult, so he picked one out at random.

Then he set to to work out a rhyme which would repair the damage that had been done.

One really has to admire him. It would have been so easy for him simply to run away from the trouble that surely lay in store for him. But this thought never entered his head. He felt that he had a duty to sort out the mess which had been caused by his inability to control the strange powers at his command.

Fortunately it was still very early in the morning and there was no traffic. No one but the unfortunate Mr Birkenshaw was yet aware of such strange happenings. The Kirbys, the Spencers and all the other folk who resided in Juniper Avenue were still blissfully asleep, and the jangling of alarm clocks had not yet called them from their slumbers.

At last Issi selected a rhyming couplet

from the jumble of writing in front of him. He manœuvred himself into a comfortable position from which he could see the results of his efforts, and without further ado read out the couplet:

"All previous magic please delete.
Bring back the Martins' house complete."

He then plucked up all his courage, guessed a number and filled in the magic card. Again there was a blinding flash which made him blink, and a huge cloud of green smoke billowed from the concrete footings where the Martins' house had once stood.

Now quite unbeknown to Issi the number which he had filled in the first magic square that morning had been correct. That is why his magic had been so devastatingly accurate. The Martins' house had indeed been "cleaned right out". It had been cleaned right out of existence.

The chances of him guessing correctly again were indeed remote, and alas the number he put in his second square of the morning was wrong.

The result of this error was not immediately apparent. At first as the green smoke thinned it seemed as if all was well. As the smoke lifted Issi saw clearly the Martins' ground floor. It looked exactly as he remembered seeing it when he got up that morning. Then the first floor came into view as the whirling smoke drifted clear of the bedroom windows.

Issi gave a great sigh of relief. He had succeeded in spiriting the Martins' house back to its rightful place.

But alas, the calm that descended upon him did not last for long. As the smoke drifted away it became apparent that the Martins' house had not been returned in its entirety.

Issi began to sense that something was wrong when he found himself checking the contents of the loft. He could make out the tailor's dummy, the suitcases, the water tank, the sewing-machine, and a standard lamp, all clearly silhouetted against the blue of the morning sky.

It didn't take him long to realise what was missing. The web of triangular timbers, the tiles and the chimneys – all were missing, laying bare to the skies the contents of the Martins' loft. The house had no roof.

Funnily enough, Issi was not unduly worried. As far as he was concerned, things

were decidedly better than they had been. What he did not realise was that to someone who had not witnessed the complete disappearance of the house, the fact that it now had no roof was in itself cause for the greatest alarm.

Mr Birkenshaw drove into Juniper Avenue with his passenger Constable Pinks. His eyes swept along the familiar row of houses, seeking out the gap where Number 41 used to stand.

Constable Pinks, for all his trained alertness, was not ready for what happened next.

Mr Birkenshaw's milk float began to hiccup as Mr Birkenshaw's right foot pumped the accelerator in a most erratic way. At the same time the float swerved.

There are not many lamp posts in Juniper Avenue but unfortunately one stood exactly in the path of the hiccuping, swerving milk float.

Alarm clocks were not needed that morning in Juniper Avenue. The sound of seventy gallons of milk, two dozen yogurts, and fifteen dozen eggs hurling themselves to the pavement amidst a shatter of tinkling glass brought everyone, without exception, to their bedroom window.

Mr Birkenshaw had seen the one sight he had dreaded to see – the Martins' house. It stood where it had always stood and the sight of it was too much for him. First he felt a little faint. Seconds later he passed out. He sat slumped over the steering wheel oblivious to the falling milk, oblivious to P.C. Pinks toppling on to the grass verge and oblivious to his audience at their bedroom windows.

The problem of the missing house was thrown from P.C. Pinks' mind at about the same time that he was thrown out of the milk float by the impact of the lamp post. He lay on the ground for a moment mentally checking every part of his body to ensure that everything was still in working order. Then satisfied that he had no violent aches or pains anywhere, and aware that several folk clad in dressing-gowns were hurrying towards the scene of the accident, he slowly got to his feet, dusted himself down and picked up his helmet. He was about to put his helmet on when he noticed a strawberry yogurt had spread itself over the inside lining so he prudently held it in his hand. That was a problem to be dealt with later. There were more urgent things afoot.

"I wonder if you'd be kind enough to phone for an ambulance," he asked politely of the first pyjama- and dressing-gown-clad figure to reach him. It was Mr Kirby.

"Certainly, certainly," said Mr Kirby and ran back to his house.

Others were busying themselves around the slumped and unconscious body of Mr Birkenshaw.

"I wouldn't move him if I were you," advised Constable Pinks taking command. "If there are any bones broken we could do more harm than good."

Mr Spencer removed his dressing-gown, rolled it up to make a pillow and gently slid it under the milkman's head to make him a little more comfortable.

P.C. Pinks was busily writing in his note-book.

"Have we any witnesses to the accident?" he asked.

There were no witnesses. They had all been asleep until the noise of their morning pintas being spread over the neatly kept verges had awoken them.

Mr Kirby came panting back.

"I wonder if you'd mind phoning the dairy?" asked P.C. Pinks. "I think the sooner they clear this mess up the better."

Mr Kirby panted off to his house again, glad to be of such assistance but wishing that P.C. Pinks had thought to mention it when he'd made the request to phone for the ambulance.

The ambulance came and took the still unconscious form of Mr Birkenshaw off to hospital. A breakdown vehicle came from the dairy and dragged the dented float away, leaving a man to clear away the debris. P.C. Pinks returned to the police station convinced that poor Mr Birkenshaw hadn't been very well at all that morning. "Good heavens above – a missing house," he muttered to himself, "whatever next. I ask you, whatever next?"

The inhabitants of Juniper Avenue, already delayed in their morning activities, were busy eating breakfast and setting off for work.

The fact that number 41 remained roofless went unnoticed.

Chapter 10

A problem more serious than a bunged-up overflow pipe

Issi was quite unaware of the fracas in Juniper Avenue of which he was indirectly the cause. He was thinking, and thinking very hard. He didn't know whether to try yet a third piece of magic in an attempt to restore the missing roof, or to leave well alone – that is, if "well" could be the word for a roofless house. It really was a problem.

He busied himself getting breakfast, but his mind was not on the task in hand. He poured the hot milk, which he had heated for his coffee, over his cornflakes and made them disgustingly soggy. He sprinkled sugar, intended for his cornflakes, over his toast and marmalade. And he put tea in the coffee percolator. His breakfast was not a success. And to make matters worse he had no licorice shoelaces left.

"There's no doubt about it," he muttered to himself as he rummaged round the sweet tin, "I do my best thinking when I'm chewing a licorice shoelace."

The Martins' roofless house stood there, completely unnoticed, until three o'clock in the afternoon. It really is a sad reflection on people's powers of observation that it was not noticed sooner.

In fact it was Mrs Spencer, a local schoolteacher and not given to hallucinations, who noticed it. She had just mown her lawn and tidied up one of her herbaceous borders in the front garden when she absentmindedly looked up at the Martins' house. There was Mrs Martin, standing on the top of her house silhouetted against the afternoon sky. Of course it was only a split second later that she realised it could not be Mrs Martin. After all Mrs Martin was not given to standing on top of her house in the afternoon – particularly without her head and legs. No, it was the tailor's dummy which had caught her eye. It was shaped like Mrs Martin because she it was who used it to fit and tack her summer dresses together, but that is where the likeness ended.

Mrs Spencer immediately called on Mrs Kirby to verify the strange sight, and

Mrs Kirby telephoned P.C. Pinks.

It wasn't until the constable heard Mrs Kirby reporting a missing roof that the events prior to his accident in the milk float came back to him. First Mr Birkenshaw and now Mrs Kirby – what was happening in Juniper Avenue today?

P.C. Pinks was on his bike and standing with Mrs Kirby and Mrs Spencer, plus three more ladies who had been called to witness the extraordinary sight, within seven minutes of receiving the call.

"But if it has just fallen off – where's the rubble in the garden?" Mrs Gray was reasoning.

"Perhaps it's been taken away," offered Mrs Young.

"Then where's the mess it made when it fell into the garden?" asked Mrs Robinson. "The garden looks immaculate to me."

The ladies, and the constable, had to admit that they could think of no natural reason for the roof's disappearance.

"When are the Martins due back?" asked Mrs Gray.

"Today," said Mrs Kirby.

"Well, they're in for a surprise," said Mrs Robinson.

And apart from Mrs Spencer's comment that it was a good thing it wasn't raining, no one had anything to offer which was even remotely constructive.

From six o'clock onwards the menfolk began to arrive home from work, and there was a constant group of people staring at the Martins' house, each making guesses about how it had lost its roof until they ran out of ideas and were reduced to facetious comments about Mrs Martin's shapely figure as represented by her tailor's dummy.

The Martins' homecoming should have been one of the most exciting ever recorded, but alas it passed so uneventfully that it really deserves no comment whatsoever.

They arrived home at half past midnight, when all the neighbours had gone to bed. The Martins were tired after six hours of driving. Issi was asleep, having finally resolved to do nothing about the roof. And it was dark.

Mrs Martin made the usual noises about "home sweet home". Claire was carried, still sleeping, from the car to her bed, while Andrew and Sally, who woke just to stagger up the garden path, decided it was too late to see Issi that night.

By half past one Mr and Mrs Martin were in bed and the only comment worthy of note was the last one that Mr Martin made before turning over and shutting his eyes.

"Good night, my dear," he said to his wife. "It's good to be under a solid roof once again."

This was reference, which Mrs Martin grasped at once, to the fact that for two weeks the family had been camping under canvas in Cornwall.

The next day was Saturday, and on Saturday morning the Martins usually had a lie in until about eight o'clock. It was to be expected that on this Saturday morning in particular the family were well set to lie in until nine o'clock or even later, so when Mr Martin was awoken by droplets of water bouncing on to his face, he was horrified to see that the time recorded by the luminous dial of his bedside alarm clock was only four-thirty. As well as water dripping on to his face he was aware of the sound of rain pattering on to the windows. Obviously the window was open too wide and the rain was driving in. He turned the light on and sat up. A drip plopped down his neck. He looked up and the next drip caught him in the right eye.

A patch of grey dampness covered almost the entire bedroom ceiling. Mr Martin was suddenly very wide awake.

"What on earth's the matter, dear?" mumbled his wife.

"The water tank must be overflowing in the loft," said her husband urgently. "The overflow pipe must be bunged up."

He grabbed his dressing-gown, made for the trap-door to the loft, and pulled the extending ladder down, congratulating himself on the instinctive alertness which, even though he was so sleepy, was prompting him to do all the right things in an emergency.

Quite naturally the water pelted through the open trap-door. This was to be expected.

Mr Martin forged his way upwards, squeezed through the trap-door and into the loft. It was then, as he stood there in his dressing-gown in the pouring rain and driving wind, that he realised the problem was far more serious than a bunged-up overflow pipe. There was a flash of lightning and he pinched himself to make sure he was awake. He just could not believe the sight

which that flash of lightning had revealed to him.

"Evelyn, Evelyn," he thundered through the open trap-door. "Come quickly – Evelyn."

Mrs Martin sat bolt upright. Hearing the terror in her husband's voice, she jumped out of bed and ran on to the landing, followed by Andrew and Sally. All three stared up at Mr Martin's drenched features looking down at them from the loft.

"The roof's gone," he said, "the roof's gone!"

There was a pause followed by an

incredulous "WHAT!" from Mrs Martin. But she could see from the rain beating down through the trap-door and on to their upturned faces that her husband was right.

After a moment's stunned silence, the Martins retired to their lounge for a warming cup of coffee, and a quiet attempt to reason out the mystery of their roofless house.

The upstairs ceilings were saturated so Claire had to be moved, but she slept through it all. The gentle lifting from her cot and the equally gentle resettlement admist blankets and soft rugs in the playpen downstairs did not disturb her slumbers. For the rest of the household there could be little thought of any more sleep for the rest of the night, although by six o'clock all were nodding in a strange twilight doze where they sat in the lounge.

Chapter 11

An Englishman's home is his castle

The neighbours each in turn awoke on that Saturday morning and looked out to make sure they hadn't been dreaming the events of the previous day. There stood the Martins' house, still roofless.

The time was nine-fifteen in the morning.

"Well, if you don't wish to report the matter officially," Constable Pinks was explaining to a very tired Mr Martin, "then there's nothing much we in the force can do about it."

"I . . . I . . . I . . . that is . . . we," began Mr Martin, trying to grapple with his thoughts.

"I may tell you sir," went on P.C. Pinks helpfully, "there's no need to say anything at the moment. Perhaps when you've got over the shock and had time to think it all out you would like to give us a ring at the station."

"Thank you. Thank you very much.

I'll do that," said Mr Martin, and closed the front door.

The excitement of the night's adventure had momentarily made the Martin family forget all about Issi, so when a few minutes later there was a gentle knocking at the back door and there he was standing in the passageway, it was like the reopening of a chapter in their lives which had happened years before. "Why of course – Issi!"

"I didn't knock sooner," Issi was saying, "because I guessed you'd all want a good lie in. Did you have a good holiday?"

This was a question with which they were usually besieged when they returned from holiday, but somehow they just weren't ready for it this time.

The conversation switched immediately to the roof, or rather the absence of the roof, and the Martins were soon hearing how it had all happened.

"Well surely," Mrs Martin was already reasoning, "surely you could magic our roof back for us, Issi."

"It's certainly possible," Andrew chimed in. "But you know that Issi's magic relies on arithmetic and unfortunately he's not very good at it and no one is allowed to help him. He has to do it on his own."

"Yes, he really ought to have some arithmetic lessons before he tries his hand at any more magic," said Sally. "I'd feel much happier about letting Issi loose on his magic cards after he's practised his counting a little more."

"That's all very well for you, young lady," said her father, "but it's going to cost me a small fortune to replace a roof. I really don't see what is to be lost by asking Issi to have a go. Goodness me – another storm and the entire upstairs will need repairing. I dread to think how much it's going to cost to redecorate the ceilings even now."

"Well fortunately," said Mrs Martin, "all the upstairs rooms badly need redecorating anyway. It was just as well we didn't have them decorated before this, er, this little accident happened."

"I have made a decision," announced Mr Martin positively. "If Issi is willing to try his magic again I shall certainly abide by what happens. Let's face it, to have a roof of some sort must be better than having no roof at all. I am all in favour of Issi having a go. It couldn't be worse."

Issi wished Mr Martin hadn't said that last sentence. After all, he knew it could be far worse. They could have been houseless, let alone roofless. No, it was hardly a very convincing vote of confidence in his ability. It seemed that his services were being called upon merely as a desperate last measure. However, he was very pleased not to have to make the decision himself, and all at once he saw the golden opportunity which was being presented to him. He now had the chance to seal the whole episode with a happy ending.

"I'm sure I can do it," he said suddenly feeling more confident than he had felt for a long time.

"And we are sure you can do it as well," confirmed Mr Martin. "Let's see if you can conjure up our roof before lunch. No time like the present."

"I know I shouldn't say this," said Sally, "but I'd feel much safer if I wasn't in the house when Issi casts his spell. You know, just in case . . ." she added.

Her father grasped her meaning at once but so as not to disillusion Issi about their confidence in him he said, "I think we'd all like to join Issi in the garden and er . . . actually see for ourselves if it works . . . I mean see it *as* it works – actually see our new roof materialising as it were before our very eyes."

Issi bundled off to his tree house to work out his rhyme and select his magic card. The card he chose looked like this:

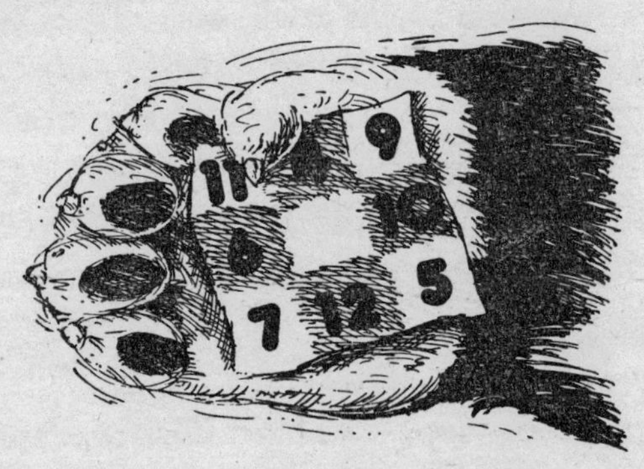

He studied it long and hard.

He now felt so confident that the sums did not seem nearly so confusing as the previous ones had done.

"Mm," he said to himself, "that looks easy enough. Now for the rhyme."

He reached for several sheets of paper and a pencil and the next hour and a half were spent in perfecting the rhyming couplet which was to establish him as the cleverest panda in the world.

"How are you making out?"

It was Andrew, unable to contain his curiosity any longer.

"I think," said Issi with dignity, "that I have the very spell to provide your family residence with the roof it deserves."

"Yes," said Andrew doubtfully, "well, don't try anything elaborate. The roof we had before will do very nicely, thank you."

"Please inform your family," said Issi, his confidence simply oozing, "that if they care to join me in the garden in five minutes I shall be ready."

Andrew ran back to the house with the message, and long before five minutes were up the Martins were assembled in the garden, fingers crossed, ready and waiting.

Issi appeared to be in no particular hurry. He joined the eager family at the allotted time.

"Bear, bear – bear, bear," cried Claire excitedly and Issi played peek-a-boo with her behind her father's back, while the Martins waited on tenterhooks. At last Issi decided the moment had come.

"Now if you'll all stand well back," he said, "I shall begin."

He plumped himself down on the grass and took the magic card and pencil from his pouch. Then he spoke the following words with all the pomp and ceremony he could muster:

"Oh magic of thyself give ample proof,
Restore to Mr Martin's house a noble roof."

He was particularly pleased with the words "thyself" and "noble". He thought they added just the right amount of dignity to the proceedings. He even glanced round to see what impact the words might have on his audience, and Mrs Martin, sensing that he was looking for approval, smiled and nodded, although it was rather a strained sort of smile.

Then, with a flourish, he wrote the number eight in the centre square of his magic card.

There was a blinding flash and immediately the top of the Martins' house was shrouded in billowing green smoke.

Mr and Mrs Martin could scarcely believe their eyes, nor in fact could Mr and Mrs Spencer, Debbie and Sarah, nor Mr and Mrs Kirby, Paul and Mark, nor Mr and Mrs Gray and their children, nor Mr and Mrs Robinson and their children – for truth to tell, Andrew had not been idle during the hour and a half which Issi had taken to work out his spell. He had told the whole neighbourhood that however surprised they had been by the mystery of the disappearing roof, that was as nothing compared to what was about to happen later that morning. And sure enough everyone in Juniper Avenue had selected a keen vantage point from which to observe the next "happening" at the Martins' house.

The green smoke slowly abated in a whirling mist of haze and there, crowning the Martins' desirable homestead, was indeed the "noblest" roof imaginable.

To the left the most perfectly proportioned and symmetrical Norman tower rose majestically above Mr and Mrs Martin's bedroom. Crenellated stone ramparts ran the entire length of the house. There was even a spiral stone staircase which would enable the occupants to climb easily to the topmost battlements, from where they would surely enjoy the finest and most commanding view of Juniper Avenue.

It was indeed a "noble" roof, transforming the house in one magical moment into the very phrase which Mr Martin so often

voiced when filled with patriotic pride, as he was from time to time, "An Englishman's home is his castle."

It is difficult to appreciate fully the deep and mixed feelings which this novel sight induced in the Martin family, not to mention the dumbfounded audience.

True, Mr Martin had a roof to his house again – but what a roof.

The blinding flash and the billowing smoke had made Claire cry, and Mrs Martin used this as an excuse for not voicing the first opinion.

Andrew was working out where he could tip boiling oil on to the heads of the attacking armies as they scaled the bathroom drainpipe.

Sally's immediate and practical worry was that the stonework looked incredibly heavy for the Bedfordshire brickwork to hold up for very long.

Issi stared in wonder and amazement. It was the most beautiful, solid and noble roof he had ever seen, and he awaited in silence the acclamation he felt sure must come his way at any moment now.

"It certainly has character," said Mr Martin, slowly and deliberately collecting his thoughts together. "It certainly has character."

Issi didn't receive the outstanding praise for which he waited that morning, but on the other hand he didn't receive any criticism either. Congratulations were subdued but encouraging.

"At least you guessed the correct number," said Sally, looking at the card Issi had completed. "Well done."

"I think the choice of the word 'noble' was probably a little too grand really," said Andrew. "Very good," he added quickly as he noticed Issi's slightly crestfallen face, "but just a bit too grand."

Certainly it was a good roof. It was a roof constructed to withstand the impact of cannon balls, and so the likelihood was that it could withstand anything the weather in Tracey Wick was likely to throw at it.

Mr Birkenshaw, head bandaged, was soon back on his milk round and was relieved to see that the Martins had after all been having some structural alterations made to their house. "So," he comforted himself, "I didn't imagine all of it!" And very soon his cheerful references to "Filling the moat with milk", and "Don't drop the portcullis on my toes, Mrs Martin", became part and parcel of the Martins' everyday life.

Constable Pinks did not receive an official complaint about the roof, for which he was very thankful and merely confined his comment to the fact that he wished he knew how the Martins had managed to get planning permission for such a violent modification.

The Martins became local celebrities overnight, and because they never told anyone exactly how it had all happened there remained an air of mystery about them which they gradually came to revel in. They intended Issi to magic the original roof back one day, but for the time being they were happy to live at "Martins' Folly", as their house became known.

Several nights later, when the first excitement had died down, Issi lay on his comfortable bed looking through his window. He was vaguely wondering if there were any pandas on the moon when he became aware of a warmth and a contentment he had never felt before.

He remembered his bewilderment after that first mysterious flash and puff of green smoke in China, and how very lonely he had felt as he camouflaged his tiny packing case home in Coppins Wood. He remembered wondering where he was and how hard he'd tried to think of something to say to Andrew when he first saw him. He remembered the misery of his sogginess when Andrew and Sally rescued him, and the nagging worries of his rather unpredictable magic.

But now, bewilderment, loneliness, misery and worries were a thing of the past as he lay there secure in his little house with so many friends near at hand.

He yawned.

"If I was searching for a word to

describe how I feel, now, at this very minute, that word would be 'tranquil', he said to himself as he snuggled away at a bump which had somehow appeared in his mattress. He yawned again. "Yes, that's it, 'tranquil'. I feel completely tranquil."

And that was the last thought he remembered thinking before falling into a very cosy and very peaceful sleep.

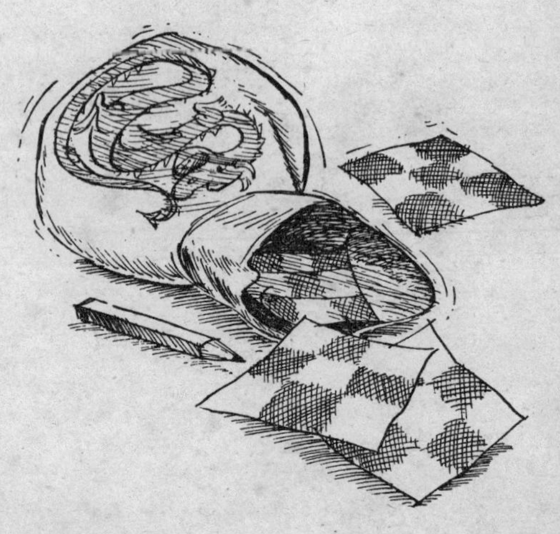